M000084156

A Sure Grip for a Wild Ride

Frank Friedmann

Evergreen
PRESS

A Sure Grip for a Wild Ride
by Frank Friedmann
Copyright ©2000
All rights reserved. This book is protected under the copyright laws
of the United States of America. This book may not be copied or
reprinted for commercial gain or profit. The use of short quotations
or occasional page copying for personal or group study is permitted
and encouraged. Permission will be granted upon request. Unless
otherwise identified, Scripture quotations are from the New
American Standard version of the Bible.

ISBN 1-58169-042-8
For Worldwide Distribution
Printed in the U.S.A.

Evergreen Press
An Imprint of Genesis Communications, Inc.
P.O. Box 91011 • Mobile, AL 36691
800-367-8203
Email: GenesisCom@aol.com

TABLE OF CONTENTS

ACKNOWLEDGEMENTS

With special thanks to the doctors, nurses, and therapists at:
Woman's Hospital, Baton Rouge, LA
Our Lady of the Lake Hospital, Baton Rouge, LA
Neuro-Therapy Specialists, Baton Rouge, LA
The Baton Rouge Clinic Pediatric Group
Children's Hospital, Seattle, WA

Thank you for your love and care of not only Avery,
but the whole Friedmann family.
You have been wonderful!

To Dr. Mary Laville,
words can't express how much
we thank you and love you!

To the body of Christ in the United States and around the
world but specifically at Quail Ridge Bible Church,
you have been available vessels
for the life and love of Jesus to flow through to us.
We are grateful!

With special thanks to
Emily Fose, Pres Gillham, and John Russin
for your free flowing but gracious red pens.

INTRODUCTION

The book you are about to read was a painful one to write because it was so painful to experience. There is no doubt in my mind that if I were able to change what my family had to experience in the last two years, I would do so in an instant. Shattered dreams can be devastating, and a silent heaven excruciating. In the traumatic times of life when darkness invades the normal family experience, hope can be elusive and faith so difficult to maintain.

In this little book, we have sought to honestly share the pain we experienced as we were confronted with painful circumstances that we could not change. We cried...we hurt...we were angry...we were fearful...and we questioned *why*. But as our circumstances confronted us, our faith confronted our circumstances. We knew that God loved us. We also knew that God is all-powerful and could do anything. Why then, were we experiencing such pain?

Some have sought the quick and easy explanation that any bad experience in life comes to us from Satan. Others have offered the suggestion that the pain we experience is simply the result of living in a world that is under a curse. These explanations are given in an attempt to defend God's reputation, but in reality have the exact opposite effect as they rob God of His sovereignty and love.

The truth is that God sits on a throne, not on a heavenly grandstand. The truth is that God could have stopped what has happened in the life of our family, but chose not to. That, in turn, means that there must be a purpose in the pain we are experiencing—a loving and good purpose. My friend, Jack Taylor, put it this way, "God is willing to look bad, in order to bring us into good." Our only response is to trust Him in the midst of pain with an honest faith. We are to trust that He *will* accomplish His eternal purposes for our lives as He provides us with all we need in the midst of our struggles.

As you journey with us in this book, my prayer is that you will find renewed faith and confidence in the God who reigns over the universe with love in His heart for you and a plan for your ultimate good.

DEDICATION

This book is dedicated to
Avery Micah Lynne Friedmann.

It tells her story, the story of a beautiful little girl
whose traumatic entrance into this world
not only rocked the lives of her parents,
but also touched the lives of an untold number
of other people as they embraced her
personally and through prayer.
We invite you to share in her first year
with the hope and prayer
that you will receive a renewed faith
"In the God of all comfort, the Father of all mercies."
We would also invite you to pray for her,
as her story is still being written.

I also dedicate this book to
Janet, Les-Leigh, Benjamin, and Morgan.

Your courageous, but childlike faith
is such a ministry to me.
It is a blessing to share life with you.
Thank you!

Chapter One

A Desire Fulfilled

Baby number four was almost here. For as long as I can remember, Janet and I had desired to have four children, a desire we thought for many years would go unfulfilled. After the birth of our second child, Janet became seriously ill. Her pituitary gland had ceased to function properly, and we were told that she could never have children again. After five years, we finally surrendered to the inevitable and canceled our maternity insurance. Three years later, to everyone's amazement, child number three arrived to be a part of the Friedmann household. Father had healed Janet, and we were so thankful to receive His marvelous grace.

Though we enjoyed our three children immensely, there was a deep sense in both of us that the Friedmann quiver was not yet full. The longing for a fourth child would not go away, even though we had yielded that desire to God. With our doctor's approval of Janet's health, we received the blessed news in April that number four would arrive in early January. Though certainly not how we had intended, with so many years between our children, God had fulfilled the desire He had planted in both of our hearts.

Since this was to be our last child, Janet and I decided to find out the baby's gender prior to birth. We had waited to be surprised for the three previous children, but this time wanted to experience what it was like to know during the pregnancy whether the baby was a boy a girl. Number four, however, would not cooperate. We tried on two separate occasions in the fourth and fifth months to determine the gender of this child, but each time number four had its legs crossed. I suggested that this child had the stubbornness of its mother and the modesty of its father, but could not find many people to agree with that.

As the pregnancy progressed, Janet began to sense that something was wrong. The baby did not seem to be moving as much as the other three had. We were told not to worry— something all of us, as parents are prone to do. The ultrasounds had been normal, the heartbeat was strong, and all looked great. We were told that the lack of movement was probably a blessing, for it appeared we were getting a laid-back, easy-going number four (something we could use with three other kids in the house and our rapidly progressing ages). Since the checkups all continued to produce normal results, we did indeed seek to accept and rest in what they said. But as we prepared for the arrival of this long awaited fourth child, Janet continued to have that motherly anxiety that all was not well.

Something's Wrong

In the seventh month, I suggested that Janet book an appointment with Bonnie, a friend of ours who does ultrasound imaging. We would once again try to determine the gender of number four. After all, our philosophy has been that the key to successful parenting is to be as tenacious as our children are. Perhaps we would finally find number four without its legs crossed.

Not long into the ultrasound, Bonnie informed us of the good news that number four was a girl. Being the thorough technician she is, Bonnie continued to check on the rest of the baby. To our layman's eyes, everything looked as normal as before. Bonnie's trained eyes, however, found a serious problem—extremely dilated loops of bowel. She told us to call our doctor and set up an appointment to do some further checking. When we called our doctor, we learned that Bonnie had already called her. There was little doubt in our minds that this was an act of urgency on her part, and we began to worry. The next day, after a short visit with our doctor, we were hurried to the perinatologist's office.

Naturally, we were alarmed and nervous for little Avery Micah Lynne Friedmann (she was no longer known as "number four"). But we were also confident that with the quality care she would receive in this age of modern medicine, she would be just fine. However, after the perinatologist did his own ultrasound, he informed us that in addition to the dilated bowels, Avery had a clubfoot. Since she had multiple deformities, he believed she was a chromosome 13 or 18 child. We had never heard such words before. They sounded ominous and burned deep into our souls...

"What does that mean?" we asked.

"It means that what she has is incompatible with life." He must have read the shock and confusion on our faces as he quickly reiterated, "She won't be able to survive outside the womb!"

She won't be able to survive outside the womb! Though the words were hollow and empty, they kept reverberating over and over in my mind. I really don't remember what we said or did next. Did we cry? Did we deny? Question? Were our heads lowered in silent prayer, or were they lifted in agonizing uncertainty toward a heaven that seemed so silent right now? I only remember the doctor's brief attempt at comfort, as he suggested that he might be wrong.

He might be wrong! We clung to that possibility. The only sure way to know was through an amniocentesis, whereby a sample of amniotic fluid around the baby is withdrawn from the mother's womb for genetic testing. This would determine conclusively if there were chromosomal abnormalities. The test, however, came with a potentially dangerous complication. Janet might prematurely deliver, and at seven months we could lose Avery.

The doctor went on to explain that if the test came back positive, it offered us the choice of terminating the pregnancy. This meant we could try again for a healthier number four. That, we informed the doctor immediately, was not an option. Being Christians, our conviction from the Scriptures was that Avery had become a person at the moment of conception. It was our intention before our God to receive her as a person, no matter what problems she had. After brief prayer, our hearts were in firm union that we would proceed with the amniocentesis in order to prepare for what lay ahead for us and for Avery.

Chapter 2

Emotional Rampage

Numb! Raw! Confused! Hurt! Time and space do not allow me to communicate all of the emotions that surged through our beings that morning. We had waited so long for this precious life and had seen God so miraculously meet the desire of our hearts. Now the very real possibility of having that desire be destroyed and our dreams shattered seemed so cruel to us. It felt as if someone had ripped precious parts of our souls out and stomped on them. It felt like someone had put our guts in a blender. *It wasn't fair. It just wasn't fair.* We said it to each other. We said it to God.

I took the rest of the day off from work to try somehow to comfort and encourage my sweet bride. The shock was so great, however, that to this day I don't remember what we said or did. I suppose we just took up space on this planet without even realizing where we were or what we were doing. Finally, it was time to get our two older children, Les-Leigh and Ben, from school. As I drove to get them, I pondered how to share the news with them. Over the years, they had often asked, "Why won't God give us another brother or sister? It's not a bad thing we're asking for, it's a good thing." When we had told them we were pregnant with Morgan, #3 child, and then Avery, they had cried tears of joy. I wondered at the kind of

5

tears they would cry now. Though the doctor could be wrong and it was possible that this could be medically corrected, we were determined not to hide the reality of our pain from them. They needed to learn, just as much as we did, what it means for us to live in a sin-cursed world and trust a God whom we cannot see. They had to be told—but how?

Faith!

As the day wore on it became clear in my heart what to do. That night, as we gathered on the living room floor to read the Bible, I had my son read from Exodus 4 where God says, "Who makes the dumb, or deaf, or the seeing, or the blind? Is it not I, the Lord?" We all needed to know that though we couldn't understand it right now, this was not some cruel accident. God was in control and that meant there was purpose in this pain. There was loving purpose from the hand of a Father who loved us enough to send His Son to die for us.

Then I had my daughter read from Deuteronomy 32:39 where God says, "It is I who put to death and give life. I have wounded and it is I who heal; and there is no one who can deliver from My hand." When they finished reading these verses and we had discussed their meaning, my son Benjamin, ever the inquisitive one, asked, "Why are we reading these verses?" They obviously recognized that these were not the norm of our Bible reading. As we looked into their questioning eyes, the tears began to form in our own. We explained to them that Avery was very sick. We told them we had been to see the doctors and that they did not think Avery would be able to live on her own once she came out of Mommy's tummy. We told them that we had taken the test to see if the doctors were right, but it looked like we were not going to be allowed to keep her as a part of our family.

6

Instantly our oldest child Les-Leigh said, "We need to pray that God will heal her!"

"That's good," I told her, "The verses we just read teach us that God heals. But what if God says no and doesn't heal her?"

Almost as quickly as the words left my mouth, Benjamin said, "Then we'll take her any way we can get her!"

As the tears now flowed freely down our faces, I broached the supreme question to them, "But what if Father says NO, that we can't have her...that He wants her to come home and be with Him?"

With all the emotion of the moment, I don't really remember which one responded first. It really doesn't matter because the others quickly agreed with the response. All I remember are the incredible words I heard from the lips of a child, as they expressed faith in a Father whose ways are sometimes hard to understand: "Then we'll let her go!"

Through quivering lips, and in between irrepressible sobs, I was somehow able to tell them that we needed to pray those things to Father. We all gathered around Mama, laid hands on her tummy, and then their young and tender voices poured out those three prayers to God. "Father, please heal her! If You don't heal her, we'll take her any way we can have her! But Father, if You want her to be with You, then we'll let her go!"

What can I possibly say to express what I felt at that moment? To see my children express such faith in the midst of such pain and confusion was overwhelming. I cannot adequately describe the "peaceful pain" we all experienced that night. It seemed as if our Father literally reached down with all that He is and hugged us as we all hugged each other. Nor can I describe the intense satisfaction amidst the uncertainty we were facing that night as I watched those little ones put their hands in God's and walk by faith. I am so thankful for the heritage of Jesus that is being built into this family. I can only wonder at how He will magnify the life of Christ in these kids as time progresses. Only eternity will reveal the impact this will have on their walk. I am so thankful that we did not seek to shield them from this pain.

Waiting

Two agonizing weeks went by as we waited for the test results. During this time, the thought of having waited so long for a baby, only to have it taken away, gnawed at our souls. Why hadn't Father just removed the desire for that fourth child? Why allow the baby's conception only to take her away? Why allow the anticipation, joy, excitement, and all those other things that expecting parents experience? It all seemed like such a cruel joke, only we weren't laughing.

Finally, the two weeks were up, and we headed to the doctor's office. With cautious hope we waited in the examination room for the doctor to arrive. Each passing minute seemed like an hour as we held each other and silently waited. As he entered the examination room, our hearts began to race. I could literally feel my heart pounding as the agonizing announcement was about to be made. He was thankfully brief: "I was wrong! There is no chromosomal damage!" The words echoed in our hearts as the veil of gloom lifted and together we cried tears of great joy. The great sense of relief we shared nearly buckled our knees. "To be quite honest," he added, "I am very surprised. I really expected the worst with what I saw on the ultrasound." We were exuberant and told him in no uncertain terms how glad we were that he was wrong!

There was little time to celebrate though, as we instantly settled in to the need at hand. Janet would need to carry the baby as long as possible so the lungs could develop; while at the same time, the doctors would closely watch the intestinal problem, making sure that they didn't rupture. This involved three trips a week to the doctor's office to be monitored and for ultrasound imaging. The game plan appeared to be that when the baby was born, she would likely need immediate surgery to correct whatever was causing her bowel to dilate.

She would also need a subsequent orthopedic surgery to correct the clubfoot at a later date. Though we would face some obstacles in the near future, tragedy had been avoided. As a family, we had received some rays of light in the midst of what had been a potentially very dark circumstance, and we praised God together.

The weeks seemed to crawl by as we were trying to keep our little sick baby inside the womb for as long as possible. With just three weeks to go to full term and the bowel continuing to dilate, the perinatologist was growing concerned. He wanted to take the baby by Caesarean section, pending the results of a lung test. This involved another one of those dangerous amniocentesis tests. Having carried the baby another five weeks, though, there was a much greater chance of survival should the test cause a premature delivery.

Later that day we were dismayed to learn that Avery had failed the lung test! She was not yet ready to enter this world. We had fully expected to be in the hospital and delivering her in a day or two. Now we were going to have to wait two more agonizing weeks for further lung development, knowing that the threat of her intestines bursting was looming ever larger. That night, however, Avery had plans of her own—Janet's water broke. Because she was in a breech position, the perinatologist recommended a Caesarean section. In his opinion, there were just too many unknowns with her, and he did not want to risk turning her in the womb.

As the doctors worked to bring Avery into the world, Janet and I clutched our hands. We have a great relationship with

Janet's obstetrician (a wonderful lady who had worked with Janet throughout her previous illness and subsequent recovery). As the procedure progressed, she kept us informed of what was going on, and we bantered back and forth as we normally do.

Suddenly, the conversation grew ominously quiet. There was an uncomfortable air in the delivery room as Avery finally entered the world. She had the most beautiful face, but something was desperately wrong. She was quickly taken to another room where the neonatologists took over. We later learned that in addition to the bowel problem, there was not one but two clubfeet, her little hands and legs were crooked, and her joints were frozen, making her unable to move. After a few brief seconds of saying hello to our new daughter, we watched as she was whisked off to the neonatal intensive care unit (NICU). Soon afterwards, Janet was wheeled to her hospital room, where uncertainty and despair once again settled into our souls.

Janet Meets Her Baby

Later that morning, doctor after doctor came to our room with questions of family history and of the pregnancy itself. As the grueling day wore on, I stayed by my bride's side while the doctors worked on Avery in the NICU. During this time one of the doctors, knowing I was a pastor, pulled me aside to suggest that if we practiced infant baptism in our faith, I should do it quickly. The implication was obvious! In at least one doctor's opinion, Avery was not expected to live. In the state she was in, I secretly wondered if that would not be a better thing for her. She looked so sad, so weak, and so uncomfortable. We hurt for her. We hurt for ourselves. All we could do in the time between the doctors' visits was sit in silence and weep.

Late in the afternoon, one of the doctors told us that the radiologists were convinced that Avery's intestinal tract had burst. The pediatric surgeon on call, herself a Christian, said she had prayed about Avery's situation and did not believe her bowel had ruptured. In her words, "They have their pictures, but I have the patient." She then presented us with two options: We could have them operate immediately and try to fix whatever was causing the swelling, or we could wait for the other surgeon previously scheduled to do the surgery later that evening. We made the difficult decision to have them operate immediately. I then wheeled Janet up to the NICU to hold her long-awaited little baby and give us an all-too-brief five minutes of bonding before Avery was whisked off to surgery.

Words are inadequate to describe the face of my sweet bride as she strained in her wheelchair to see this precious little girl who had entered our lives so tumultuously. On her face was a look I had seen three times before. It was the look of a proud mother anxiously waiting to see her baby for the first time: the look of longing that can only spring from the love of a mother's heart. But there was something different this time. The look of longing was mixed with more than a trace of fear at what she was about to see. As the nurse gingerly picked up Avery, with all the tubes and wires connected to her little, twisted body, the tears streamed down Janet's face. The pain in my sweet bride's heart swept across her face as she reached out her loving, tender arms to hold this precious little gift from Father's hands for the first, and possibly the last, time. From her devastated heart, she spoke through trembling lips as she looked up at me and said, "She's like a little broken doll!"

Surgery

Janet could only hold her for a minute or two as the surgical team prepared quickly and was soon ready to operate.

11

Time had become an enemy, and the doctors decided they had to operate at once. We briefly prayed for her, yielded her once again into Father's hands, and surrendered her into the arms of the nurse. And then, as we had done so often with this child, we waited. Father had answered the first facet of our family's prayer: He was not yet going to heal her from her affliction. We, for our part, had fulfilled the second facet of our prayer: We had indeed received her regardless of her condition. Now we wondered in fear and sorrow if the third facet of our children's prayer was going to be answered: Was He going to take her away from us so soon? And we waited...

After several hours, the doctor entered our room to share with us that it was intricate surgery, "much like operating on an earthworm." We learned that there had been a five-inch blockage between her small and large intestine. This, in turn, had caused the intestinal tract above the blockage to dilate and prevented the intestinal tract below the blockage from developing properly. After removing the blockage, the doctor had to make something like a funnel from the extremely dilated small intestine to the atrophied large intestine.

Then came the glowing report we had so desperately hoped we would hear: The operation appeared to be a success. She would have to be watched very closely to make sure the newly created funnel would not develop a blockage, but the intestinal tract above and below the funnel would eventually return to normal development. This meant a lengthy stay in the NICU, but it appeared that Avery had come through with flying colors and was here to stay. "She proved to be a real fighter" was the assessment of one medical practitioner. Little did we realize how much of a fighter she was going to have to be.

Chapter 3
Searching for Answers

Over the next several days, we were continually barraged with various specialists whose job it was to determine what had happened to this sweet little girl with "normal" ultrasounds. Finally, we were informed that the consensus among the doctors was that Avery had a rare disease called Arthrogryposis Multiplex Congenita. This was actually just a description of her multiple, stiff joints which had hindered her movement in the womb. Since she had been unable to move, the confining pressure of the womb had twisted her little developing body and kept her muscles from developing normally. Because her joints had frozen into place, her bones were small and brittle. In fact, her arm was broken during delivery. Armed with this new information, we shuddered at the damage that could have occurred had her little body been forced to travel down the birth canal. We praised God for the wisdom of the neonatologist who had ordered the Caesarean section.

As we sought to sort out all this trouble that had come upon her, a question began to haunt our minds: *What about the normal ultrasounds?* Everything had looked so good and normal those first five months. The answer we were given was that her problems probably began in the fifth to sixth month. Up until that time, she had been a little girl who was developing normally.

This new insight caused floods of guilt to menace our souls mercilessly. We kept thinking, *Had we done something to cause this to happen to this precious little girl?* We racked our brains furiously to determine what we could have done. How could this happen? Janet had been so faithful to eat and drink properly, to exercise, and especially to avoid medication. *What did we do?* became the plague of our minds. The doctors assured us that this was not our fault. We heard their words and tried to receive them, but it was difficult to not feel that we were somehow responsible for what happened to Avery. Guilt, it seems, is something that registers all too easily with the human condition, and we were no exception.

The doctors further explained that there are some 300 types of Arthrogryposis, but that no one has ever been able to determine its cause. The rarity of the disease and the lack of research into the condition make the actual diagnosis very difficult to make. As one doctor put it, "This is a random freak accident in utero, and you will likely never know what caused this."

A random, freak accident? The words burned into my soul as the words I had instructed my children to read weeks before pounded into my mind: "Have I not made the deaf and the dumb?" says the Lord. No doctor, this was not a random, freak accident. We knew "Who" was behind this, and we didn't like it, nor for that matter did we like Him at that particular moment. In the brutal honesty that can only flow in a relationship of intimate love, we told Him so...

Our Special Assignment

If there's one thing the Bible teaches with absolutely no variation, it is the sovereignty of God. He rules...He reigns...He is in control! As Ephesians 1:11 puts it, "He works all things after the counsel of His own will." This does not mean that God causes evil in any way. But it does mean that He allows evil in this sin-cursed world in order to accomplish His purpose. Because of the world we live in, there are defects in the genetic makeup of man. That defective genetic makeup shows up in all of us. All we need to do is look in a mirror, and we can see it. The problem we had is that it showed up so severely in Avery.

We had to face the truth that God our Father *could have* intervened and with His glorious power and grace, reversed that defective genetic makeup. On this occasion, however, He *chose not to* intervene, and in His glorious power and grace He allowed Avery Micah Lynne Friedmann to be born with this terrible disease. The Friedmann family knew that this was no accident. We also knew that because God has revealed Himself to us as a loving Father, He was not allowing this in order to punish us. No, there was love here and a glorious purpose. In the midst of our pain, however, it was hard to see that purpose; it was hard to see His love.

During this time, *why* was a word that dominated our minds and our hearts. We now knew that Avery's intestinal problems would take time to heal, but they would heal. Her little limbs, however, were severely affected with little chance of ever becoming "normal." This painful reality mercilessly pounded our hearts every day. All around us we could see the normality of others who were enjoying their children, and that meant that every day was a new experience of loss. There would be no Avery running into our arms…there would be no little girl riding her tricycle or mastering her skates. Loss seemed to be everywhere, every day!

The morning before Janet was scheduled for discharge, she called me and tearfully said she wanted to come home. I encouraged her in the decision and applauded her courage. For her to leave the hospital (which meant leaving her baby) took a tremendous act of the will and faith in her God to watch over and care for Avery. Though my words were meant to comfort and encourage, I knew they sounded hollow to her through the pain she was experiencing. All around her, mamas and their babies were bonding together, but Janet's arms were empty.

As I drove into the discharge area at the hospital, I could see Janet in the wheelchair with her empty arms, and both of us began to cry. We couldn't help but look at the rear seat of our car where there was also an empty carseat. Having experienced three joyous going-home celebrations before, we both knew very well that what we were experiencing at this moment was wrong! This was not how it was supposed to be! Yet, somehow, in the eyes of our God, it was right. It was His plan for our baby and for us. She was our special assignment, and we were to trust Him for all that was needed to carry out this assignment called Avery Micah Lynne Friedmann, even though we did not understand why it had to be this way.

Despite our pain and all the wild emotions we were experiencing, Janet and I committed ourselves to be and to do all we could for Avery. Every opportunity was taken to visit her, but we wanted to do more than just visit her. We wanted to give her the best possible chance to walk and use her hands, so we had the therapists teach us how to stretch and exercise her little body. Everything we read on the disease said that therapy was essential for the first year. With each visit, we embarked on a regimen of stretching her stiff little body. This was no easy task. Often it would take just a touch to those tiny feet or hands to send her into a fit of crying. With all she had been through, we who were supposed to provide love and security were now bringing pain and fear to this little darling. We knew it hurt her—it hurt us as well. But true love, agape love, required that it be done. We had to give her the potential to move with the goal that maybe, one day, she would be able to walk and use her hands. So we faithfully labored over her, crying as she herself cried, until one extremely painful day.

We arrived at the hospital, as was our normal routine. As we approached the "pod" where she was spending her days, we noticed that she was awake. Her little face was filled with that angelic expression that only babies seem to be able to muster. With love in our hearts, we leaned over the crib to say hello and smile at this one who had both filled and broken our hearts. But no sooner did the words leave our lips, than her sweet countenance eroded and her face filled with fear as she erupted in tears. The reality of what was happening hit us hard. She had come to associate our voices with pain. Apparently in her mind, we, her parents, were bad news, and that broke our hearts even more than they were already broken. We made the decision right then and there that "parental therapy," though a necessity for the treatment of this disease, would not begin until we had her home. That way, we would have hours of nurturing and cuddling her to offset the periods of pain.

Going Home

After 10 long weeks, Avery had gained enough weight and her intestinal tract was working sufficiently for her to come home with one stipulation—she had to have a feeding tube inserted. She was simply not strong enough to suck a bottle sufficiently to receive adequate nutrition for normal development. It was a very difficult decision for us. Our baby was going to eat through a tube in her tummy. It just seemed so wrong, so unfair. God had given her a mouth, and that mouth was meant to nurse gently at her mother's breast. That was how it was supposed to be. For Avery, though, a tube was the only way we could get her home and have her be a part of our family. With

17

our backs against the wall, we finally relented and the tube was surgically implanted into her little tummy.

Once we got her home, we tried to regain a normal family life. For months our time together as a family had consisted of trips to the hospital. We found, however, that life was never going to be "normal" in the Friedmann home. Avery required a lot of therapy time at home and many trips to the various doctors' and therapists' offices. This consumed much of Janet's time and energy as she became nurse, therapist, and medical driver. I, in turn, became Mom's taxi as we tried to allow the other children to continue as much as possible with their own lives. It was a very difficult time, but everyone pulled together, and we began to function as a family again. As we continued to work with Avery and take her to therapy, she gradually got stronger. Her body began to loosen up, and to the amazement of everyone, she began to kick her feet and hold her head up! Though it took long hours to feed and care for her, and our lives were permanently changed, we were home. Together, we were growing in hope until...

Chapter 4

Back to the Hospital!

In early May, Avery began vomiting and developed a slight fever. With the fear that her intestinal tract had once again become blocked, we headed to the doctor. When we placed her on the scales, we were shocked to learn that Avery had lost 23 oz. in just over 18 hours, something she could ill afford, as she only weighed 9 pounds. She was rapidly dehydrating, and our doctor wisely sent us to the hospital. The nurses immediately began trying to hook up an IV to replenish her fluids but were unable to find a vein, a very common occurrence with her disease. For over an hour, little Avery endured being repeatedly stuck with IV needles in a desperate attempt to replenish her rapidly diminishing fluids. Finally, a doctor became available and swiftly inserted a deeper IV called a central line. In a short while, Avery began to look and feel better. Over the next several days, a barrage of tests was conducted to determine what was happening. The doctors suspected that the intestinal blockage had returned as she continued to have high fevers and vomiting. She was taken off all bottle feeding and put back on intravenous feeding in an effort to give her intestinal tract a rest. As each agonizing day went by, her condition progressively worsened, and we found ourselves once again settling down for an extended stay in the Pediatric Intensive Care Unit (PICU), Avery's home away from home.

One week later, on May 15, Avery's little body crashed! Whatever was happening was taking its toll, and it was several hours before the doctors and nurses were able to stabilize her. At this point, the pediatric surgeon told us that she really did not know what to do. In her words, "I'm afraid to operate, but more afraid not to." With the various lab tests and x-rays producing no results and our baby girl deteriorating before our eyes, we affirmed the doctor in her decision to operate. We anxiously waited, praying first that they could find an answer, a cause, and then hopefully a cure. Finally, the doctor appeared with "Good news and bad news!" The good news was that the original surgery appeared to be a great success, the blockage had not returned. In fact, there was no intestinal blockage to be found anywhere! The bad news was that she couldn't find anything wrong! To our prayer that we could find a cause and cure, Father had answered a resounding "No!"

"What are we going to do? What other tests can we run? We've got to do something quickly or we're going to lose her!" The questions shot out of my mouth faster than she could answer them. Worry flooded our souls along with intense feelings of helplessness. Our baby was dying before our eyes, and no one could help because no one knew why this was happening. The only One who did know, our heavenly Father, was ominously silent once again. The walk back from surgery to the PICU seemed endless as we accompanied Avery in her gurney. Once there, we spoke little, we held each other, we looked at each other and our baby with empty eyes, and then the phone rang...

A Diagnosis, A Cure

It was the lab! They had found the culprit—a blood fungus coupled with an extremely rare bacterial infection. Together they had attacked her intestinal tract and were now moving through her body attacking her kidneys, heart, lungs, and other vital organs—but there was a cure. We rejoiced at the great news we had just received, but it was bittersweet. The reality of what had just happened hammered us hard. Avery had gone through a surgery she did not need! If only the lab had found the result just two hours earlier, this precious little fighter would have had less to fight against. For reasons we will probably never know this side of heaven, Father had allowed her to endure extra pain—WHY? That word seemed to be in our vocabulary a lot. Looking back on these events, we have no doubts concerning the choice that we made to operate. Our backs were against the wall. Our precious little girl was slipping away with no understanding as to why. As her parents, it was a chance we had to take. We would make the same decision again, based on the information we had at the time. Though there are no doubts about that, there are certainly regrets. It seems so wrong to have put her through the pain of a surgery she did not have to have—WHY, FATHER? It would be asked again, all too shortly.

The Path to Healing

We were now on the path to healing. The antibiotics being administered to Avery were having their desired effect. The bacterial infection was gone, and the blood fungus was diminishing. The problem was that they were "heavy duty" antibiotics, which carried some very adverse potential side effects. "Such as...?" we asked. Brain damage and heart failure were the possibilities. Because of the seriousness of the side effects of the medication, we were told she would be hospitalized for some time. The prescribed medication would be administered three hours a day for six weeks, and they wanted to monitor her condition closely.

There was no alternative other than another long hospitalization. The doctors and nurses performed their regimen of care; and thankfully, with each passing day, Avery grew in strength. She began to take a bottle again, albeit ever so slowly. It seemed as if we were starting all over again. When she began to dehydrate she was up to almost two ounces of milk by bottle (the remainder of her milk was supplied through the stomach tube). Now we were back to measuring her milk intake by mouth with c.c.'s, but at least she was taking a bottle again.

Equally important to us was that she was fast becoming Avery again. Her engaging personality and heart-capturing smile were returning and bringing us joy once again. Very often, I would come into the intensive care unit and find nurses huddled around her. My heart would skip up to my throat and my mind would race as I quickly entertained the possibility of "Here we go again." But as I approached them and questioned if something was wrong, I would inevitably be told, "Oh no! Everything's fine. We're just enjoying her." And they were! And to be sure, she was enjoying them as well. The gleam in her eyes and the smile on her face proved that to any who passed her bedside. One nurse after another informed me that it was nearly impossible to pass her bedside without being drawn in to visit for a few minutes. One of them summed up the power of this little person who has graced our lives so dramatically. She pulled me aside one day to tell me, "Whenever I'm having a bad day, I just go visit that little girl for a few minutes, and everything just seems better." Already in her young life, Avery had a ministry.

Going Home Again?

It was so hard to believe! Could it really be true? Defying all the predictions of a lengthy hospital stay, after only 10 days on the antibiotics, Avery had become stable enough to go home. We would be receiving home health care each day to administer the remaining antibiotic treatments, and that would enable us to be a family once again. As had become our routine, that night we gathered at home with our other three children for family supper, homework, and catching up with each other's lives. Then Janet and I returned to the hospital one last time to prepare Avery for bed. Tomorrow she was coming home! We were so thrilled we could hardly contain ourselves!

When we arrived, we found her a little cranky with a slight fever. The nurse gave us her bottle and informed us that it had a new medicine in it to counteract what the antibiotics were depleting from her little body. It felt so good to be able to hold her and feed her, and just plain love her. It was a preview of what tomorrow would hold, and we cherished the moment. The moment, however, did not last very long.

Something was wrong! Shortly after finishing the bottle, Avery became clammy to the touch and began sweating profusely. We called the nurse and pointed out what was happening. Since it had happened so quickly after her feeding, we naturally questioned if it could be caused by the new medication she had been given. Perhaps she was allergic to it, or this was an expected side effect. Most likely it was simply that the fever was breaking, but we had learned with this little one to not assume anything. The nurse checked the chart and informed us that she had received the proper medication and dosage ordered by the doctor and that all was fine.

Avery, however, grew uncharacteristically cranky. It was obvious that something was bothering her. As we tried to console her and make her comfortable, she vomited. Naturally our first thought was *Here we go again.* But what could it be? The surgery had ruled out an intestinal blockage, and the powerful antibiotics ruled out any infection. We concluded that it must be the medication! We called the nurse over and again questioned her about this new medicine. She rechecked the chart and again informed us that all had been done properly.

However, we were not convinced. Over the next hour and a half, we attempted to console Avery and finally settled her down to sleep. Before we went home, we voiced our concern for a third time about the new medicine. The nurse said that if Avery did not improve over the next hour, she would cut the dose in half at the next feeding and call the doctor at home. With that assurance, we left the hospital to get some much-needed rest and prepare for bringing Avery home the next day. We held hands as we drove home, physically exhausted and emotionally drained, but wonderfully excited at the joy tomorrow would bring.

As our heads were about to hit the pillow, Janet turned to me and said, "I've got a really bad feeling about this. I can't explain it, but I feel like something really bad is going to happen." I hugged her and tried to reassure her as best I could, telling her that with all that we had been through, our emotional radar was probably searching for something further to go wrong. I reminded her of what the last six months had brought to us and that her emotions were raw from the wear. It was like being on a wild roller coaster ride that we were unable to exit. I also reminded her that this phase of that wild ride was ending—Avery was coming home! But I was wrong...

Chapter 5

We Have an Emergency

The ringing of the phone yanked me out of bed with my heart pounding and my mind racing. I guess Janet's words had left a nagging dread in my subconscious mind—*Something bad is going to happen!* I ran to the phone, and as I did, I glanced at the clock. It had only been 15 minutes since we had gone to bed. It was the hospital! The words still echo in my mind, "Mr. Friedmann, we have an emergency! You need to get back to the hospital right away!"

My words came quickly and to the point, "Why? What happened?"

The shallowness of her response communicated the seriousness of what was happening. "Please Mr. Friedmann, Avery is in cardiac arrest! You need to get here right away!"

We sped to the hospital with tears streaming down our cheeks and that empty, empty word once again crossing our lips, *Why?* We were so tired and weak, so scared and unsure of what awaited us. The wild roller coaster had picked up speed again, and as we held hands, Janet verbalized the fears our hearts shared—"Are we going to say good-bye to her now? Is this all the time we were going to have with her? Lamb, I'm not ready to let her go. I'm willing to, but I don't want to."

We prayed as we drove, once again surrendering our precious little girl into the hands of our Father, while at the same time pleading that we might be able to keep her with us. We loved her. We had received her and wanted to keep her. When was it ever going to end? Was it going to end now?

As we raced into the ICU, we were met with a team of solemn and unfamiliar faces. We would later learn that they were doctors and nurses from what is called "the crash team," who are summoned from throughout the hospital when someone is in an emergency situation. The manager of the pediatric ward approached us immediately and prepared us quickly saying, "Things do not look good, but we are doing everything we can."

While we caught our breath, we glanced around and recognized a familiar face—the chief doctor of the PICU was there. Later we would learn that he and a pediatric cardiologist had been called in to check on another baby and "happened" to walk in just as Avery's little heart stopped. Friends would later inform us that Father was really watching over her to have sent Avery these incredible doctors at just the time when she needed them. We knew that was true, but we were not much comforted by that knowledge. In our minds was the growing suspicion that the new medicine had somehow caused this latest episode. Yes, Father had supernaturally provided pediatric specialists at the moment of Avery's greatest need. But if Father would go to those great lengths to watch over her and rescue her, why wouldn't He protect her from the need to be rescued? If Father loved her so much, *why* (there's that word again), why wouldn't He protect her from going into cardiac arrest in the first place? In the deepest recesses of our hearts, we knew it was the new medication.

As we waited in the hallway so the doctors could work to save her life, we alternately prayed, grumbled, cried, and begged. I, for my part, grew very, very angry. "Not like this,

God! Not like this! On the day before she's supposed to come home, she gets killed from medication? All the miracles on her behalf, only to be taken from this world by human error in an institution of healing?" I could feel it welling up inside me, and I was ready to explode!

The arrival of our friends and the elders of our church helped comfort us greatly. These were familiar faces in a sea of strangers. Most important, they were mature Christians of faith who allowed us to grieve without trying to "fix" us. They also allowed us to be angry, without trying to correct us. They were there—as those who tried to understand what we were going through—but realized they could never, ever feel what we were feeling. That realization was perhaps the greatest thing they could have ministered to us. They gave us the freedom to feel the completely normal feelings of hurt, anger, and anxiety that come in the midst of great pain and uncertainty. They made no attempts to do anything other than offer their support and help to us as we needed them.

The main doctor who had cared for Avery during this hospitalization then arrived. The confusion on his face nearly equaled our own. He had expected her to be going home. "What happened?" His question was quickly met by my own deepening conviction: "It's the new medication! Her heart stopped! She's dying!" No one could miss the shock on his face. His eyes grew wide and his face grew pale as he raced into the ICU. Shortly thereafter, one of our friends, himself a doctor, emerged to tell us that it was indeed the medication. Somehow a mistake had been made in the dosage calculation, and Avery had been given *five times* the proper dosage. What's worse, we found out that besides the dose which we had given her, the nurses had given her an earlier one as well, which accounted for Avery's condition when we had arrived at the hospital that evening.

As our earlier fears were confirmed, we were overwhelmed by the sea of emotions that surged through us during those terrible minutes. There were no words to speak. What could possibly be worth saying at a moment such as this? She had fought so hard. She was supposed to be coming home. But *supposed to be* and *reality* now had a huge gulf between them. We felt completely devastated, utterly hopeless, and so very, very frustrated. We simply did not have the resources within us to protect this precious little girl who had so much stacked up against her. We were forced to realize completely the sheer fantasy and illusion of what we think is our ability to control our circumstances.

At the same time, though, I found myself growing increasingly angry and ready to explode in a vain but desperate attempt to take charge of the situation. At the very least I could mete out a punishment to the offenders who had brought such tragedy to one who needed no more trauma in her life. And then...

Chapter 6

Honesty and Humility

The door of the ICU swung open and the doctor, visibly shaken, approached us. The words reverberated in my mind, though he only said them once: "There's been a tragic mistake with Avery's medicine. She's in critical condition. We're doing all we can, but she's got a long way to go. I want you to know that it's *my* fault. I miscalculated the dosage of her medicine, and I accept total responsibility for what's happened. I'm so very, very sorry."

We had just witnessed a rare event. Such integrity and character are not often found among men these days. Instantly a wave of compassion flooded over us, which can only be attributed to God the Holy Spirit working in and through us. No one can generate that kind of compassion for a man while in the midst of experiencing such great pain at his hands.

By His grace, and only by His grace, we reached out and grabbed the doctor's hand. We told him we loved him. And then we told him the most outrageous words that could be spoken by hurting human beings: "We love you, and we forgive you. Now go do everything you can to make her better." And then, as before, we waited.

A Prayer for Healing

After what seemed like an eternity, we were called in to see her. There were tubes, wires, and machines all over the room. We had been through this before, but this time was different. She was unable to breathe on her own. Her eyes were closed. Her face was tight. We could see on the monitor that her little heart was racing erratically. She was laboring to survive! With our friends and the elders of our church, we gathered around her bedside and joined hands to pray. By the grace of God, I asked the doctor to come into the unit and join us. One of our friends held his shaking hand as we waited for someone to pray…

But there were no words spoken. No one prayed. I supposed that no one knew what to say. Truly, what can be said at such a moment? In my own strength I did not have the words either, but I opened my mouth and somehow they came out, desperately hard and agonizingly slow… "Oh Father…we stand here….confused…weary…and scared. We don't understand, we really don't understand…how…or why…this happened. She's so frail…so little. Oh God…be her strength…. She needs You…. And we need You to raise her up…. Please do that for her…and for us…. Father…we thought she was going home with us tomorrow…but we'll say it again…if You want her home with You…we're willing to let her go…. Even now…we release our hold on her…and surrender her to You….She's Your baby…. But Father…she's also our baby….You gave her to us…and we'd like to keep her for a long, long time if You'd let us…. I pray You would…. I pray You'd heal her once again…. And Father…before You…we forgive the human error…and ask that You shed Your love on all of us right now…because we all need You very, very much. Thank You, Father. Thank You, in Jesus' name."

We'll See If She's Here

One of our dear friends took Janet home to break the news to the other children and care for them while I kept vigil by Avery's side through the rest of the night. Early the next morning, a crew of people came in and began hooking Avery up to a machine. One of the doctors came by to inform me that they were going to do a brain scan and see if the "event" (as it was now being called) had any detrimental effect on her. Put simply, they were now checking for brain damage. The words rang ominous in my mind. *Would brain damage be added to the list of things she was to struggle against in this world? Or was she already gone and her body would soon follow its own path to death?* The wild roller coaster was making its way to the highest peak yet, readying itself for a furious descent into where, I did not know. I alternately welcomed and dreaded the fast approaching moment when the machine would be turned on.

With the preparations complete, the doctors, nurses, and therapists all gathered around her bed and held hands. I stood beside her and lovingly contemplated this precious little girl who was now wearing wires and tubes in place of her home-coming outfit. The respirator was rhythmically doing its job. Her heart rate continued to race erratically, and her temperature was soaring! The fear of what might be ravaged my being, and I broke into tears! The doctor graciously cut short the agony of anticipation by announcing, "Well, let's see if she's here." I don't believe I've ever known a more intense moment in my life. With the flick of a switch, we would know whether my daughter was now brain dead, mentally retarded, or still the little sharpie we had come to know and love.

All eyes were riveted on the doctor as he flicked the switches and stared at the machine. I prayed silently, "Oh, please, God!" And then, without saying a word, the doctor looked up at me, lifted his hand, and gave the largest thumbs up signal I had ever seen. The room erupted with shouts of joy and praise. She was here! She was alive! And the thumbs up had to mean that there was no brain damage. *Didn't it have to mean that there was no brain damage?* His words confirmed my hope: "She's not only here, she's actively here. She has above-average brain activity. Congratulations!"

Chapter 7

A Sure Grip for a Wild Ride

W ords. They seem so inadequate here. There are not enough of them available to describe the incredible explosion that took place inside my being. LIFE! What an incredible word! Little Avery Micah Lynne Friedmann was still endowed with life! It was her gift from the Life-Giver; and as it should be, that life was fighting to live by fighting against death.

As I write now, the tears still come. What an incredible series of ups and downs this thing called life has taken us on these last few months. There have been such devastating lows that in turn have given way to such overwhelming highs. Our bodies seem hardly able to endure the physical strain. Our emotions, though incredibly active, seem to have become numb. Together we wonder how much more they can take. We wonder if somewhere there will be a breaking point, a point of no return.

I shared with our church body, as I had with Janet, that it is like being on a giant roller-coaster ride that is scaring the very life out of you, but it won't stop and let you get off. You simply have to hold on with all you've got, and here's the key:

Realize that the real issue is not that we have a firm hold on life; but that the Source of Life, who has identified

Himself as the Father of all mercies and the God of all comfort, has a firm hold on us with all that He is.

With this as our confidence, and by His grace, we can then trust Him. I put that in italics because I don't intend to pretend that this is an easy thing to do, nor is it something to be said flippantly. There is a great need to use empathy and compassion when exhorting someone to trust God, especially someone who is hurting so terribly that it feels like their guts have been run through a blender. Trusting Him, however, is the only truth path available for us to obtain the sustaining power we need when we encounter the agonies that life can throw at us. We need a *big God*, who can handle big problems. Fortunately, when we trust Him, we will find Him true to the task. His Life will remain triumphant in and through us, even when it is confronted with this world's life and all of its trials.

The Ride Continues

For the next several days, we watched Avery struggle to live. Her heart rate would remain incredibly high for awhile, only to periodically drop desperately low. She fought higher fevers than I had ever seen before. Her kidneys were not working, nor were her lungs or intestinal tract. And so we waited, as we had done so many times before. The doctors informed us that they had, in essence, done all that they could do.

Now, it was up to Avery. Would she have the tenacity to fight? This was now our greatest fear. After all, her experiences with life on this earth had not been very good thus far. We wondered if in her little spirit, she would simply decide that planet earth was just not a very good place to be. We wondered if she would decide to call it quits and go home to be with

Jesus, to a place where there is no more pain. Time would tell...and so we waited.

Four days later, with Janet and I at her bedside, Avery Micah Lynne Friedmann woke up! We greeted her with tearful smiles, which she tried hard, so very hard to return. And then, she broke into tears. How could anyone blame her? With all she had been through, I find it incredible that she even tried to smile. Avery was going to live; she was here to stay! And it didn't appear that she would suffer any permanent damage from the "unfortunate event." The light of God's grace and favor had broken through a very dark period of our lives once again.

The next week saw Avery's condition gradually improve until she was taken off all the machines. The tubes were removed, and finally, we were able to bring her home again. We gathered up her belongings and paraded out of the intensive care unit with an entourage of friends and caretakers. This time, Janet's arms were full, and the carseat had a passenger. This was the way it was supposed to be. The relief and joy flooded our hearts once again, as the roller coaster entered a peaceful portion of its track.

Chapter 8

Living as a Family

Life has become different for the Friedmann family. Physical, occupational, and speech therapy are weekly requirements as we seek to give Avery the opportunity to develop to her fullest potential. Janet has continued as nurse, therapist, and medical driver in addition to her responsibilities as wife and mother. Retaining my new role as "Mom's taxi," I have endeavored to do all that I can to enable our other children to continue with as normal a life as possible. This will be our life for as far down the road as we can see. It has, of course, been a strain physically and emotionally. Each evening brings an exhausted thanks that we have made it through another day. Each morning brings another day to trust God's strength in the midst of our weakness. We press on in this way, taking one day at a time, and are steadily becoming a family again.

Our children continue to be a great blessing as they honestly face the hardships that Avery faces. They cry and they question just like we do. But they also laugh and rejoice as we experience together the ups and downs of life in this world.

We continue to take trips to special clinics where we hope to find some answers as to what happened to Avery in the womb. Those answers will aid in determining a prognosis for her and will also help determine the direction of treatment. As it stands now, she faces several surgeries to correct her structural problems. Whether or not she will ever walk or be able to care for herself with her hands remains unknown. What we do know is that we love her greatly and are so grateful that she is a part of our family. To be sure, she came into this world and broke our hearts, but as she develops into who Father God made her to be, she fills our hearts as well.

With God's strength we will continue to fight for her, just as she herself fights to be all that Father brought her into this world to be. And praise God she is fighting. Why? Because the truth is she is not a broken doll. She is a human being—made in the image of God, fashioned to share in His glory through Jesus Christ. This we know and cling to, that one day the glory is coming for Avery Micah Lynne Friedmann. We don't see it right now, but it is coming.

Until the glory comes, though, we face a lot of uncertainties. Put simply, Avery's story is still being written. Though we don't know what tomorrow holds, we do know Who holds tomorrow. It is because of that personal relationship with God through the person and work of Jesus Christ, that our motto has become that from a recent popular movie, "We will dance again one day!" *We will dance again!*

Chapter 9

Reflections

People do not often share their intimate thoughts and personal feelings when they encounter trauma in this life, at least not with the vast majority of people. That privilege is reserved for the counselor's office or the friend's embrace. In a world where there is very little mercy and understanding, vulnerability and intimacy are shared only with those who have earned it. So why have we been vulnerable here with you? The answer is simple—we want to share with you the Life that has been shared with us.

For all of us who live in this world that is under a curse, the issue is not *if* we will encounter frustration, hurt, and broken dreams, but *when* we will encounter them. If the trials of life are not here right now, then be aware that they are coming. Perhaps they are just around the corner. That truth instantly confronts us with another issue—*how* will we be able to make it through those difficult times.

Through Avery's story, we have sought to share with you that being a Christian does not vaccinate us against the traumas of life, nor does it cauterize our emotions so that there is a perpetual silly smile on our faces. Being a Christian means that you can be real before a very real God. It means you can share your very real struggles with Him and expect a very real response from Him! That doesn't necessarily mean that He will erase your struggles, though He can and often does do that. What it does mean is that He will provide you with whatever grace you need to live through whatever it is you are experiencing.

Please understand that the reason behind this confidence we have as Christians is that the provision He offers us is Himself. Very often, when we are in the pit of despair, we look for an answer, a way of escape. When we do that, we become frustrated and overwhelmed with our burden, because most of the time there is no way of escape. There is no way to undo the trauma that has come into our lives. We must avoid the temptation to look for an answer! It is not an answer that we need, but a Person—Jesus Christ. Through the Bible we can come to know Him personally and appropriate His power to our circumstances. That is because He promises to meet us where we are, with all that He is.

If you are already a Christian and are hurting right now, please don't be religious with Him. Don't suck it up, grit your teeth, put on a happy face, and say, "Praise the Lord!" Don't pretend that everything is fine when it is not. Be honest with Him. Tell Him you hurt. Tell Him that you don't like what you're going through. Tell Him you don't understand. He is not insecure in who He is. He can receive your honesty.

But please, don't stop there. Be honest also with yourself and admit that you're not up to what you are facing because you aren't. You and I were made for a garden, a place called Paradise; and if you hadn't noticed yet, this world we live in is no garden. There are storms out there, and we need Him. Please, tell Him so. Invite Him into your trial to be all that you need Him to be. Ask Him to be God to you. That is a prayer He will always answer. Please know that His provision for you in response to that prayer may not be what you intended, but He will be God to you. He will provide you with all that He is, for all that you are going through. He will provide you with His Life for what you face in your life.

If you are not a Christian, you need to become one. I cannot imagine going through this life without the enabling power of the living God being lived in and through me. We all need Him simply because we were *designed* to need Him.

Many have commented on how we as a family have had to depend on Him in a great way. My response to them has been, "Yes, the same way that all of mankind is supposed to depend on Him." My friends, God never intended for us to live independent of Him. But when Adam cut the umbilical cord from God to man, we all showed up on this planet separated from God. The sad result of that truth is that we have all learned to adapt accordingly and live in this separated, independent state. Because we have been so incredibly created in His image, there is much we can do independent of Him. Indeed, we can be so successful apart from Him that we can even forget Him or deny that He even exists.

There are some things, however, that we cannot do because we were never designed for them. We were never designed to face death. We were not designed to handle the trauma of sickness or the ache in our souls that comes from being rejected and abused. Again, we were made for a garden paradise, and we must recognize that this world we live in is *not* that paradise. To live here in this place that can sometimes seem like a desert, we are going to need the provision of Someone who can satisfy the thirsts that spring from the deepest recesses of our soul. That is what Jesus offers to do for all who come to Him. That is what He will do for you if you will trust Him.

That is precisely what He has done for the Friedmann family. He met us in our anger, and gave us an awareness of His presence within us. This assured us that we were not going through this alone. He met us in our frustration and disappointment and provided us with His peace that gave us the courage to face another day. As each new sunrise brought another tremendous need for strength, He met us in our weakness and proved Himself sufficient for our needs. In the midst of what seemed to be endless hurt, He provided us with a confident expectation that life would be good again. It would be different—not what we would have chosen, to be sure—but it would be good. The Friedmann family experienced God as He proved to us the truth of what He said in establishing the new covenant: "I will be their God and they will be My people."

I hope you can see that this is the only plausible explanation for what occurred in the PICU the night Avery was given the accidental overdose of her medicine. It was not the power of my wife and me that enabled us to love and forgive that very human doctor. Nor was it our ability to have great faith. What it was, my friend, was the life of Jesus Christ being lived on this planet, just as sure as it was lived 2000 years ago. The only difference is that His life was now being lived through normal, everyday people through the glory of the New Covenant, which God established through the person and work of Jesus Christ. It is this same life that He offers to you if you will but trust Him to do so.

Some have said that Jesus is a crutch. I used to argue against that, but I no longer do so. A crutch is exactly what all people need. A crutch is a support that holds up a person who is weak, and we are all weak human beings. Dear one, if you will but admit you are weak and trust Him Who is strong, He will hold you up. That's why He died for your sins—not just so you and I can go to heaven—but so He can bring heaven to us, by living inside us right now. I pray you would invite Him into your life so that you may find Him to be what we have found Him to be—faithful!

For information about Frank Friedmann's ministry call:

LIVING IN GRACE

Voice Mail: 1-800-484-2046 then dial ext. #9506

or visit our website at:

www.livingingrace.com